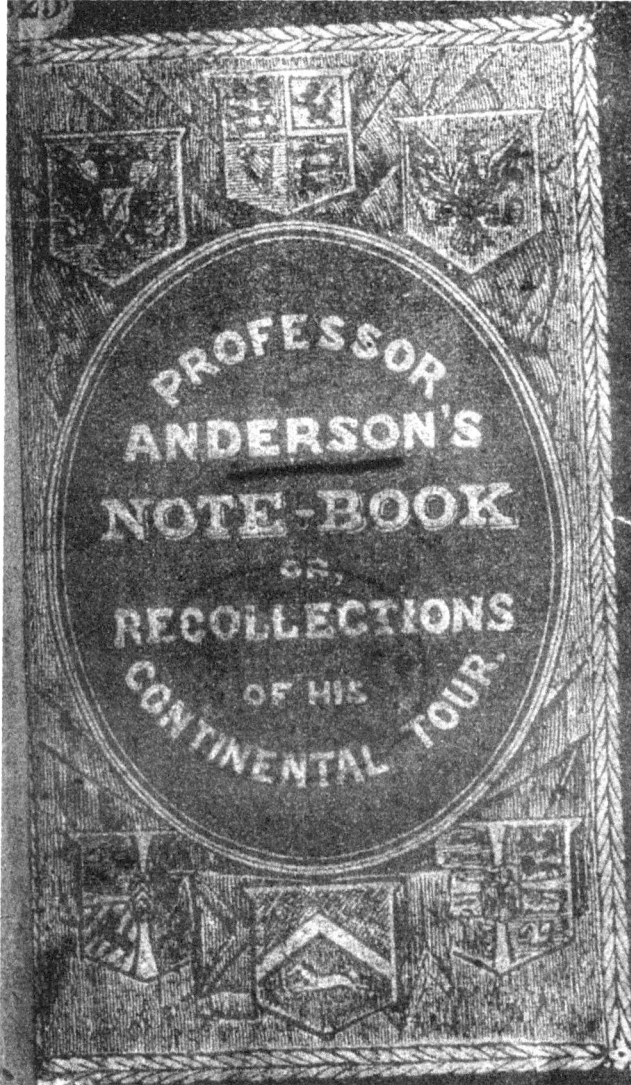

PROFESSOR
ANDERSON'S
NOTE-BOOK
OR,
RECOLLECTIONS
OF HIS
CONTINENTAL TOUR.

ADDRESS.

—o—

PROFESSOR J. H. ANDERSON takes this opportunity of returning his most sincere thanks to the hundreds of thousands of patrons who have honored his Magic Temple with a visit, and to inform them that his means of entertaining the public has no limit, as his experiments in natural magic ranges through the whole field of the sciences, and have been witnessed by the whole of the Monarchs of Northern Europe, in addition to the most prominent Professors of the learned Societies.

In presenting the following romantic sketch, Professor J. H. A. begs to assure his readers that it is a veritable account of what actually took place during his sojourn at Brechin Castle, and can be noblemen and gentlemen then resident in Saint Petersburgh. In conclusion, Professor J. H. A. begs to state that the present sketch is but one of numerous incidents and reminiscences of his Continental Tour, and that he intends, from time to time, presenting his patrons with similar records of his visit to the Continent, forming, when completed, a Bijou Volume of Facts.

PROFESSOR

ANDERSON

AT

BRECHIN CASTLE.

FROM THE

Note Book of the Wizard of the North.

PROFESSOR ANDERSON

AT

BRECHIN CASTLE.

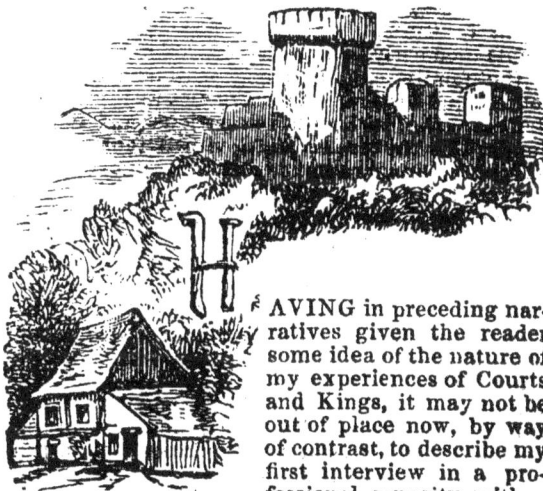

H AVING in preceding narratives given the reader some idea of the nature of my experiences of Courts and Kings, it may not be out of place now, by way of contrast, to describe my first interview in a professional capacity with a lord — a real living hereditary lord of our own country. Before doing so, I may explain that, like my father before me, I am a born Scotchman, and

as two or three cities have (or ought to have) laid
claim to my place of birth, it may be as well to
enlighten the public on this important point as to
that part of Caledonia in which I first saw the light.
It was in a very small cottage on the estate of
Craigmyle, in the parish of Kincardine-O'Neil,
Aberdeenshire. My father was by trade an ope-
rative mason, which he followed in the city of
Aberdeen. He had a "large small family" as the
saying goes of twelve of us to support, your humble
servant being the oldest, and I may at once here
frankly confess that whatever may have been
my alternations of fortune since, I was neither
nursed in the lap of luxury nor idleness. My
parents died early, which had the effect of breaking
up the family, and I, along with sundry little
brothers and sisters, was entrusted to the care of
relatives, who, although industrious and careful
enough, like the tender and loving parents we had
lost, could not afford to keep us long out of employment. Accordingly, so early as ten years of age I
was sent out to battle my way in the world without
a guide or director. I became what is termed call-
boy in Mr. Ryder's theatrical company, which then
used to go the round of the northern circuit, and
continued with that gentleman for several years,
in the course of which I picked up a knowledge of
men and things, which oftentimes has stood me
in good stead. It was here I first imbibed the
rudiments of the art of which I am not an un-
skilful professor, and laid the foundation of my
somewhat eccentric, but not unpleasant or unpro-
fitable career. I had an opportunity of seeing the
celebrated Ingoldby perform his necromantic
tricks, and having a natural turn for mechanics, I
set my brains working, not forgetting my hands,
and in a short time succeeded in making a number

of curious specimens of mechanical apparatus in a rude style, by the help of which I sometimes managed not only to deceive my friends, but astonish myself. About this period I had the offer of other employment of a more permanent and perhaps more profitable description, but having once come fairly in contact with the foot lights and rubbed against scenes and side-wings, theatricals and their accessories became my hobby, and have ever so continued.

The public are already aware of the immense sums which from time to time I have expended in theatrical speculations, and in particular of my last, but not least unfortunate of all, the Glasgow City Theatre. And here I might not inopportunely comment upon the fate of that magnificent structure, its equal not to be found in any town out of the metropolis, the hopes which it created in my bosom, the run of success which accompanied my management of it, and the ruin which it involved on my prospects, when I stood in a state almost bordering upon frenzy, and beheld the ravages of the flames until the once gorgeous walls were a mass of blackened ruins. But I am digressing, but I dare say the reader will forgive me. I set out with the intention of describing my first interview with a lord, and now to my tale. At the age of 17 years I left the company of Mr. Ryder and commenced on my own account my present profession, which I have successfully pursued in Scotland, England, and Ireland, and over a great part of the continent of Europe. I made my *debut*, however, in a few of the smaller towns in the immediate neighbourhood of my native place, where my anticipations of good fortune were more than realised. In the course of this early tour, 1 called at the town of Brechin, where I engaged the Farmer's

Hall for the purpose of giving my entertainment. When here I took up my quarters at the well-known Swan Inn, which was then kept by Mr. M'Bean, a bit of a wag, and quite a character in his way. After the first night's performance I was honoured by a message from Brechin Castle, to the effect that Lord Panmure desired an interview with me, previous to my giving a private exhibition before a company then staying with his lordship at the Castle. I had often heard of Lords, Dukes, and Earls, and had even seen Kings and Queens in the Theatre, but the idea of coming in contact with the genuine article in the way of business, had never once crossed my fancy. Burns' description of his feelings on being invited to dine with Lord Daer, conveys something of what were mine on that occasion. It was—

> " A ne'er to be forgotten day.
>   Sae far I sprauchled up the brae,
>   I dinner'd wi' a lord."

But as old M'Bean remarked there was no help for it, so I mustered a sufficient stock of courage, and went down to the Castle, where, on telling my errand, I was at once ushered into the presence of Lord Panmure, whom I found to be just an ordinary looking mortal like myself—for

> " The fient a pride, nae pride had he,
>   Nor sauce, nor state that I could see
>   Mair than an honest ploughman."

His lordship received me most graciously, told me that he was that night to have a large party, and desired to know if it would suit my convenience to give my slight-of-hand exhibition before them. I

managed, in reply, to stammer out, "Y-e-s, my
lord;" when he remarked that I had better make
my preparations immediately, and showed me into
the library, which he said he would reserve for my
use. Having bowed my acknowledgments, I was
making my way into the hall when I encountered
Lady Panmure, to whom his lordship called as I
was passing along—"Lady Panmure, tell the con-
juror to come and take dinner with us to-day,"
upon which her ladyship, in the most courteous
manner, intimated to me his lordship's wish. I
thanked her ladyship, and made my way out of
the great house in the best manner I could, and
hurried back to the Swan in a state of fear and
anxiety, such as I had never previously experienced.
M'Bean, the landlord, observing my agitation, and
being anxious to ascertain my reception at the
Castle, eagerly inquired what had taken place,
when I informed him that his lordship had sum-
moned me to give my entertainment that night to
a large party, and, what was worse, I had been
invited in the afternoon to dine there; and never
having seen a real living lord before, much less
dined with one, I was quite at a loss what to do or
how to conduct myself. "Hoot, man," said
M'Bean, "there's nothing sae easy; ye maun list
keep your e'e on ilka body, and dee as ye see ilk
other folk deeing, and if there's fifty dishes on the
table ye maun taste of them all, and see that ye
leave naething on your plate." He further instructed me that "if my lord or my lady should
ask you to tak' a glass o' wine wi' them, be sure to
say, 'Weel, my lord, y'er guid health;' and if there
should be a heap o' leddies in the drawin'-room,
and you see yin waitin' without a gentleman, ye
maunna tak' haud o' her airm, but jist march on
before her into the dinin'-room, for fear her guid

man may be angry wi you; for," he added, "these
great folk, ye ken, are awfu' jealous o' their better
halves. With these, and a few such hints and
advices anxiously administered by my waggish
friend, M'Bean, whose true character at that time
I was in ignorance of, I set about preparing my
apparatus for the evening. I got the whole completed in a short time, and returned to dress for
dinner. Having completed my toilet, I made my
appearance before M'Bean, who again rehearsed
his code of instructions, at the close of which he
suddenly exclaimed, with an air of astonishment—
"Preserve us man, ye'er no gaun in that coat?"—
(I had on a plain dress coat)—"That's not a coat
tae gang tae a lord's table in." I said, "is it not

the fashion?" "Fashion!" exclaimed M'Bean "wha ever heard o' a body gaun to a lord's table in a dress coat? Ye maun get a frock coat to be in the fashion." I informed M'Bean that, unfortunately, I had not such a thing about me. "Never mind," said he, "I'll lend you ain." I thanked him kindly for the offer, and he immediately sent up stairs for his Sunday frock coat, which was a very excellent black one. I may inform the reader that M'Bean was rather a corpulent stalwart person, and I was not then full grown, and rather lanky. However, I made a fair exchange, and donned his frock coat, observing that I thought it rather large for me, but he declared with great seriousness that it fitted me like a glove. Being fully accoutred to his satisfaction, off I started for the Castle, where I arrived half an hour before dinner. I once more took a look at my apparatus, to see that all was right, and was then shown into a room where there was a large party in waiting. As I entered all eyes were directed towards me, as if I had been the lion of the evening, and I took a seat in a corner of the room to avoid observation. Upon looking round I was somewhat surprised to find that every gentleman present wore that sort of coat my friend had advised me to put off, and that I alone had on a large frock coat. I consoled myself with the reflection, however, that M'Bean, in his anxiety for my welfare, had committed some mistake. By and by, after we had waited a short time, several of the gentlemen approached me, and having introduced themselves, said, "Well, Sir, I suppose you intend to astonish us to-night;" to which I answered, "Yes, I will if I can." At last a servant announced that dinner was on the table, when the whole party stood up and proceeded to the dining-room. I, of course, remained until towards the last, when I and a lady alone were in the room. Faithful to M'Bean's advice, I did not offer her my arm, and we stood looking at each other for a few seconds. At last the lady said, "Mr. Anderson, I'll take your arm," which she did in a moment, and led me to dinner. I do not know when I felt or looked so sheepish. No sooner had I got to the table than I seated myself down on a chair, and in order to keep pace with M'Bean's views of the customs of the great, I left my fair partner to do the same. At first I trembled lest I should commit

some gross mistake at dinner, but after the two
first courses I made myself quite at home, and
most religiously followed the advice of my friend,
the innkeeper, as to leaving nothing on my plate,
until I found that M'Bean's coat was not too large
for me. Most assuredly I *astonished* them. There
was not a person at the table with so good an
appetite. While dinner was going on, my Lord
Panmure said, " Mr. Anderson, I will be happy to
take a glass of wine with you," to which I promptly
replied, "Well, your very good health, my lord!"
The whole party looked at me, and then smiled to
each other. They evidently soon discovered that it
was my first appearance at the table of a lord, and no
doubt thought I was fair game for their waggery.
They all drank wine with me; and, still following
the directions of M'Bean, I drank "good health"
to every one round, until I began to feel the effects
of the generous liquor in my head. Dinner ended,
the ladies rose to retire, when, not forgetting
M'Bean's good counsel, I got up and went along
with them, amidst a burst of laughter, which I
was then somewhat at a loss to understand. Lady
Panmure and her female friends proceeded to the
drawing-room; and observing me looking rather at
a loss how to act, her ladyship, doubtless with the
view of keeping up the joke, beckoned me to go
along with them,—a signal which I promptly
obeyed. Here I seated myself down, but on looking round felt a good deal surprised that the other
gentlemen had not followed my example. Being
a little elevated with the wine, I asked Lady
Panmure for an explanation, when she observed
that there was nothing wrong, and that she hoped
I would make myself quite at home. The request
was made in such a courteous and familiar tone of

address, that I found no difficulty in obeying it. Here, surrounded by a bevy of beauties, I was induced to give Lady Panmure an account of my birth, parentage, and education, in the midst of which a messenger from Lord Panmure announced that Mr. Anderson was requested to prepare for his entertainment. On this I went to the library, put my necromantic apparatus in order, and in a few minutes afterwards had the honour of appearing before Lord Panmure and his party, whom I was fortunate to surprise and delight by a few of my magical experiments. All expressed themselves pleased and astonished, and at the end of my entertainment I was invited to supper. In the interval, Lord Panmure's steward, who was in attendance at table, and seeing me young and inexperienced, very kindly took me aside, and having ascertained that I had been following the burlesque directions of M'Bean, gave me a few hints, by which I was enabled to cut a more creditable figure at the supper table. I took my leave of the Castle that evening much better pleased with myself than I was at the beginning, and still more so when next morning I received from his lordship an envelope containing a ten pound bank note (the first which I had ever seen), and a letter, of which the following is a copy :—

Brechin Castle, 12th March, 1831.

Sir,—Your performance last night at Brechin Castle much delighted myself and party. You far excel any other necromancer that I ever saw either at home or abroad.

I am, Sir, yours, &c.

PANMURE.

with this money, which was the foundation of **my**
fortunes. I started on my present profession, resolved to carry it out. The remainder is perfectly
wellknown to the public.

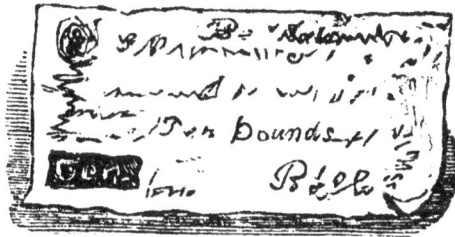

PROFESSOR

ANDERSON'S

FIRST INTERVIEW

WITH THE

EMPEROR OF RUSSIA.

FROM THE

Note Book of the Wizard of the North.

PROFESSOR ANDERSON'S FIRST INTERVIEW WITH THE EMPEROR OF RUSSIA.

THE incidents connected with my introduction to the Emperor of all the Russias, and the occasion of his Majesty afterwards presenting me with some handsome testimonials, although scarcely so romantic as those which led to my interview with Jenny Lind's mother, in Stockholm, are somewhat amusing, and may bear repetition. I need not take

up the time of the reader with a narrative of my
journey to the capital, or with the preliminaries to
my being permitted to perform there after my
arrival, suffice it that I obtained the use of the
Alexandrisky Theatre for the purpose, and, as
usual, astonished the natives with my experiments
in natural magic. Russia, I may here observe, is,
a country that, of all others, abounds with extraordinary sights, some of which are sufficiently
striking, and invariably attract the attention of the
traveller. Among these I may mention their
masquerades, my attendance at one of which I
have reason to remember as long as I live. These
public entertainments in St. Petersburgh, or rather
promenades, as they may more appropriately be
called, generally take place in the Nobility's Hall
or Bolchoi (great) Theatre. On the night of the
masquerade an opera is usually given, and the
Theatre then is attended by the nobles, the
officers of the Court, the merchants and civilians
of all classes, and from almost every quarter of the
globe, and at these displays one seldom fails getting
a sight of the Emperor. I may remark, *en passant*,
that so perfect and powerful is the machienary of
the Theatre that in less than an hour after the

opera is over, the stage, orchestra, scenery, and pit
are removed *en masse,* so that the house is at once
converted into a magnificent hall for the reception
of the maskers. The company in most cases begins
to assemble about twelve o'clock on masquerade
nights, and the parties present continue walking
up and down the hall, gossiping, love-making, or
conversing over the affairs of the day until they
retire to their respective places of abode. The
ladies, by the way, are alone privileged to wear
masks on such occasions, and of these, it is said,
they sometimes take an undue advantage, Be this
as it may, when a masquerade night is announced
in St. Petersburgh, strangers are always on the
qui vive of expectation, for it is there where the
manners and habits of the Russians in public may
be observed to most advantage. To such an opportunity I was privileged shortly after my arrival,
in company with my friend, Mr. Maynard, an Eng-
lishman, who volunteered to be my *cicerone* to the
place. At the close of my entertainment on the
appointed evening, I was accordingly joined by my
friend, who accompanied me to the Bolchoi Theatre
to see the masquerade. We got there shortly after
the hour of meeting, and such a sight for grandeur

and magnificence I never witnessed either before or
since. On arriving at the entrance, we suddenly
emerged from the comparatively darkened street,
and walked into the theatre, with its tiers of boxes
and splendid decorations, lighted up with ten thousand wax tapers (a spectacle at any time calculated
to astonish and confuse the beholder) and after ad-
vancing a few paces, I found myself in an assembly
of from four to five thousand persons of varied
ranks and conditions, and dressed in every variety
of costume to be found from the borders of China to
the banks of the Neva. There were Tartars, Cir-
cassians, Cossacks, and Russians, military officers,
(whose numbers preponderated) of every grade,
besides Englishmen, habited in the plain black
dress which I generally wear. Ladies with and
without gentlemen, promenaded through the room,
diamonds and jewellery blazed on every side, and
music lent its inspiring influence to the scene. To
say that I was surprised, pleased, delighted, would
convey but a faint idea of my feelings at the time;
I was absolutely bewildered, and kept moving
through the crowd gazing around me, and paying
but little attention to the hints and advices which
my more experienced friend was pouring into my

ear. I could recollect, however, at one time, that Maynard, amongst other matters, was very busily engaged informing me that the Emperor was in the room, and that although there were from a thousand to fifteen hundred military present, no one was entitled to recognize him. and for any one to do so was considered such a gross breach of etiquette, that the offender was invariably punished; when I suddenly, by accident, came right against a gen-

tleman in front of me, dressed in full military
uniform, to whom I at once turned round and
apologized for my awkwardness, at the same time
humbly craving his pardon. The gentleman did
not seem to be half pleased with the encounter, but
bowed and passed on without remark, when, to my
horror and astonishment, Maynard exclaimed,
"Gracious powers, what's this you've done, Anderson? You have not only jostled the Emperor's
person, but addressed him publicly, in direct viola-
tion of a well-understood rule in Russia;" my
apology, in his estimation, being worse than the
offence. Of course I was aware of the law on the
subject, although not acquainted with the person
of the Emperor, and I can assure the reader that
after this mishap, my admiration of the fine things
in the hall that evening very speedily gave way to
an entirely different feeling, and my fears were
nowise abated when friend Maynard pleasantly
inquired if I had ever heard of such a place as
Siberia, and followed up his query by advising me
to go and pack up my traps immediately, in case
the secret police should be at my lodgings ere I got
home, to do it for me. After keeping me in a state
of agonizing suspense for a few minutes, Maynard

tried to console me with the reflection that in all likelihood the Emperor would forgive the offence on the ground of my ignorance of the customs of the country; and so, to my unspeakable satisfaction, it afterwards turned out. We had taken a few more turns of the room, conversing about my unlucky casualty, when I again got a look of his Majesty, whom I found no difficulty in recognizing this time, and more especially as I observed him directing the attention of a gentleman who was along with him, to your humble servant. At the close of the masquerade, I made the best of my way home in a frame of mind not to be envied, and notwithstanding the merriment of my companions, who now began to talk of the affair as unworthy of serious notice, I slept little that night. When I did get a short interval of rest, visions of Siberia, the knout, imprisonment, whipping, and the interior of mines for life, flitted across my brain, and I awoke in a state of feverish anxiety, which was broken upon on the morning of the following day by a message from the Emporor, addressed to "Bolchoi Focoksnick," (the Wizard of the North). When I opened the packet, I trembled from head to foot, but on reading, my terror changed to an

opposite sensataion, when I found that it contained
an order, commanding my presence to perform
before the Emperor in his winter palace. I need
scarcely say that on the day appointed I hastened
with pleasure to fulfil the commands of his Majesty,

who, along with the Empress and the members of
his court, appeared at the entertainment, and
seemed highly gratified with my experiments. One
of these that most astonished the Emperor was what
I term my illustration of "second-sight." So
surprised was His Majesty with my description
of things invisible, that he began to fancy that I
had confederates in his own court : and in order to
test my powers, he abruptly asked me if I knew
what sort of watch he had in his pocket? when I
promptly replied, "Please your Imperial Majesty,
nothing is more easy. Your Majesty's watch is a
gold one—it has one hundred and twenty brilliants
around the centre, and on the back of it there is an
enamelled portrait of your father, the Emperor
Paul." His Majesty and the Empress laughed
heartily, and admitted the accuracy of the description. In order further to convince His Majesty
of my necromantic skill, I informed him, to a
second or two, the precise time which his watch
indicated ; and what appeared more extraordinary
still, I informed him that he would find the
watches of every member of his court standing at
the same time, with the exception of that of the
Empress, which had not gone for fifty years. It, I

explained, was worn more as an ornament than for use, and was a relic of Peter the Great, to whom it originally belonged—to the truth of all which His Majesty graciously nodded his assent. At the close of the entertainment, the Emperor, who speaks English fluently, politely asked permission to examine my apparatus—a favour which I was only too happy to grant. On coming upon the stage, His Majesty looked at the different articles which I had made use of with much interest, and was pleased to compliment me on the ingenuity of their construction. In the course of his inquiries, he told me that when a young man, he was very fond of these amusements, and, in fact, had himself been an amateur magician. While travelling among the Kirgees—a people who inhabit a tract of country between China and Russian Tartary— he had learnt, he said, one trick in particular, as to which, in return for the information I had given him, he would initiate me. That experiment is the same that I now perform at the close of my entertainments. My tutor in it was the Emperor Nicholas, who, along with it, presented me with the splendid magician's dress which I am now proud to wear. and which is essential to the proper accomplishment of this particular trick.   In conclusion, I may just inform the reader that my first meeting with the Emperor ended not only in my obtaining the patronage of his Majesty to my entertainments, but also that of the entire Court at St. Petersburgh, which was a little more to my wishes than a visit to Siberia.

LUDICROUS INCIDENT

THAT OCCURRED TO

PROFESSOR

ANDERSON

WHEN

IN IRELAND.

FROM THE

Note Book of the Wizard of the North.

PROFESSOR ANDERSON
IN IRELAND.

N peregrinating through the small towns of Ireland, my assumed designation of the " Wizard of the North" occasionally made me a partaker in scenes which, for extravagance and absurdity, I am sure could have occurred in no other quarter of the world but the Emerald Isle. Some of these were attended with accidents and mishaps sufficiently annoying at the time, but, in general, they afterwards turned out to my advantage. As an illustration, I may relate one adventure. While travelling from Clonmel to Waterford, I had arranged to stay a night in the little village of Carrick-on-Suir, at which place I arrived late in the afternoon of an extremely cold day in the month of December.

At the time to which I refer, there were no railways in Ireland—so, for the sake of convenience, I drove my own carriage, a machine by which I could easily convey from place to place my apparatus, and all the articles connected with my magical laboratory. The carriage in question, although of simple construction and unostentatious in appearance, had the capability that to me was all-important, of embracing *multum in parvo;* and when I drove up to the door of an inn it attracted no more attention than the vehicle of an ordinary traveller. On the outside, I may mention, I invariably carried my carpet-bag, umbrella, and a box in which I had Guinea pigs, rabbits, pigeons, and other live animals used in my professional operations; and these were generally the only articles I requested to be taken in doors by the

waiters. On this occasion, after rather a long
drive through an exposed part of the country, I
entered Carrick-on-Suir, half perished with cold
and fatigue, and came up to an inn, of respectable
exterior, called the " Erin-go-Bragh," the waiter
of which came to the door, and inquired if I would
have my luggage taken out. I said " No, only
part of it ;" and I explained that the articles I
wished removed were my umbrella, carpet-bag,
and the box on the top of the carriage, of which
I instructed him to take especial care, and see
that he did not turn it upside down. With these
instructions, and my horse and machine put up
for the night, I entered the inn, and was politely
received by the landlady, who, after the customary
greetings, at my request showed me the warmest
room in the house, as I had been suffering from a
severe cold for a few days previous. It was a neat
little parlour, right over the kitchen, where, after
ordering tea, I sat down to rest myself before a
comfortable turf fire. Here I must explain, that it
being a very old house, and the flooring regularly
washed for half a century, the boards had got
opened, and the ceiling not being plastered below,
I could hear distinctly every word that was spoken

by the parties in the kitchen. Accordingly, I had
not been long in my new quarters until I was
privileged to hear the following dialogue between
the hostess and her waiter :—" Paddy," said she,
after a pause, " What gentleman is that up stairs,
that belongs to the horse and the carriage ?" to
which he replied. " I don't know, ma'am." " Is
he a commercial traveller, do you think ?" . " Commercial! did you say ? Who ever heard of a commercial traveller carrying live stock wid him ?—
Why, ma'am, there's something very mysterious
about his whole appearance. His carriage is the
most infarnal-looking machine I ever saw, and
there's a mystification around him that id' puzzle
a parish priest." " Live stock !" exclaimed the
landlady. " Yes, ma'am, shure when I tuk his
box off the top av the carriage, didn't I turn it
upside down, and then I heard out of it the most
unarthly squeaking ye's ever listened to. Bedad,
ma'am, I'm afeared the gentleman is not at all
what he pretends to be." At this recital the
curiosity of the landlady was aroused, and she again
asked—" Paddy, who do you think he is at all ?"—
Sorry a bit ma'am can I guess who he is. Shall I
go up stairs and ask the gentleman's name and pro

fession?" "O no," said she, "that would be bad manners, Paddy, but really I should like to find out who he is." "Well now," rejoined Paddy, "a thought strikes me, I know how I'll find him out." "How will you do it?" said the landlady, eagerly. "Why, ma'am, I'll fetch you the gentleman's umbrella, and isn't there a little plate on the handle, wid some writin' on it that'll may be tell you all about him." "That was well thought of, Paddy," said she, "just run and fetch it here." The suggestion was no sooner made than acted upon. In a twinkling, Paddy had the umbrella out of the stand in the lobby into the kitchen, and all hands

were called into requisition to help to make out the characters on the little plate, which, being in old English, gave the party some trouble to decipher. After a good deal of bad spelling, and some rough guesses, "Pat," said the landlady, taking the article in her hand, "it's a quare umbrella, after all—let's see what the name is?" She began spelling slowly W I Z A R D, and went on until, with the help of others, the full inscription was ultimately made out—"Wizard of the North."— "Wizard!" she observed. "What sort of a profession is a Wizard, Paddy?" The cook screamed out, "A Wizard's a *banshee*." "Bedad' an' your right," said Paddy. "The other day when I was at Clonmel, I heard of a Wizard, and they said he was the *banshee*, or what's worse, the devil;" and, added he, in a whispering tone, to his wondering listeners, "It's the devil, sure enough, that same gentleman in black up stairs, and these infarnal squeaking things in the box are his imps!" This discovery of Paddy's, which was explained with all the earnestness of a firm believer, had the desired effect upon his credulous auditors. The umbrella was thrown to the ground as if it smelt of brimstone, and sundry exclamations were uttered by the whole party respecting their personal safety. One was for leaving the house instanter, another for bringing in the help of neighbours, and a third for sending for the priest. After a good deal of surmise and suggestion as to the disposal of the person of your humble servant, it was agreed to do nothing rashly, but at the same time they resolved on making a careful examination of the mysterious box, to which Paddy directed their serious attention—and in a few minutes the

box was carried into the kitchen, with a view to
having a look at its contents ; and sure enough, to
my infinite amusement, I heard the cord with
which the lid was fastened unloosened, and the lid
suddenly thrown open ; when, in an instant, my
entire stock of pigeons, rabbits, owls, rooks, &c.,
flew out in all directions, to the extreme terror
of the landlady and her domestics, who, amidst
the leaping of the rabbits, the fluttering of pigeons,
and the squeaking of Guinea pigs, made their way
into the street, crying that the devil had come to
Carrick-on-Suir.   The bawling and shouting in
the street soon collected a crowd of spectators, to
whom the waiters and chambermaid recounted the
particulars about the box and the umbrella, and
gravely assured scores of open-mouthed listeners
that the devil was up stairs, in No. 5.   During the
whole of these unusual proceedings I had not
moved from my room, not knowing exactly what I
should do—when on looking out of the window
after the clamour had moderated, I observed that
the crowd outside had procured a cow-tether, one
end of which they had fastened to an old hasp in
the front door, and at the other end some forty or
fifty young and old Paddies were holding on in

order to prevent my escape from the house. In-
dividuals in the assembly ever and anon blessed
themselves, and wondered whether I would most
likely attempt the door or the window. When the
good people had exercised themselves in this way
for a short time, during which the lamentations of
the landlady were heard above the hum of voices,
some one in the crowd, more wise than the rest,
said, " What's the use holding on here? Sure if
he's the devil he can come through the key-hole!
Had'nt ye's better send for the priest?" This pro-
posal was at once agreed to, and a messenger was
hurridly despatched for Father —, a neighbouring
clergyman, to request his immediate presence at
the Erin-go-Bragh. His reverence, I must say,
lost no time in coming, supposing, I have no doubt,
that some person in the house had taken ill; but
judge his surprise when he saw the crowd in the
street holding on by the cow-tether to keep the
door shut, and a score of voices beseeching him to
go up-stairs, and lay the devil in No. 5. His
reverence, although at a loss to account for this
extraordinary demonstration, ordered the people to
let go the tether, which they did with some hesi-
tation, when he opened the door, and entered the

inn,—followed at a respectful distance by a number
of his flock, who seemed greatly alarmed for his
safety,—fearful lest the room might suddenly be
emptied of us both. Nothing daunted, however,
his reverence approached my door, at which he
gave a gentle rap, and I responded "Please walk
in, sir;" when the gentleman entered, and after
uncovering, said "Sir, I hope you'll forgive this
intrusion ; but the fact is, the inmates of this
house, through some awkward mistake or other,
have taken you for his Satanic Majesty, and the
whole village is alarmed. Will you be kind
enough to inform me who and what you are, that I
may allay their apprehensions." On this I turned
round to address his reverence, and looked him
full in the face, when he exclaimed, "What! Mr.
Anderson, is it you?" [I may here remark that
the reverend gentleman had been in Dublin when
I performed in that city, and witnessed my entertainments, and therefore found no difficulty in
recognizing me.] And he added, "Have you been
playing off any of your magical tricks here?" I
briefly explained to him the cause of the accident,
my professional name on the umbrella, the escape
of the Guinea pigs, rabbits, &c. We had a hearty

laugh over the matter, and he retired, assuring me
that he would, as far as lay in his power, disabuse
the minds of the people as to my identity with the
Prince of Darkness. I said it was a very unfortunate occurrence for me, as I had ordered tea an
hour and a half ago, and it was not yet served up;
when he observed that, from what had taken place,
I need be in no way surprised ; and he added that
I had better make no noise about it, but let the
people of the house have their own way for that
night. Of course, I had no alternative ; and after
his reverence left, with the consolatory remark,
that he hoped I would find my accommodation
better than I anticipated, I waited patiently for
about a quarter of an hour, when I could stand it
no longer. I rung the bell, and I heard footsteps
on the stairs, and shortly afterwards a voice
called through the key-hole, " Did ye's ring, sir ?"—
I replied in the same direction, " Yes, bring me
some tea;" on which the waiter departed. Ten
minutes more might have elapsed, when the door
was cautiously opened, and I looked round, ex-
pecting a person to enter with a well-furnished
tea tray ; but what was my surprise, on casting my
eyes to the floor, to find a tray walking, as it were,

into the room, pushed on by means of a long
sweeping brush, and a man's arm at the other end
of it. This part of the performance being accomplished, and the articles got into the room as far as
the brush and a man's arm could shove them, the
arm and the brush were cautiously withdrawn, the
door again closed, and the same voice cried
through the key-hole, " Help yourself, sir !"—
Under any other circumstances I would have
laughed outright, but being half famished, I did
help myself, and in this I had little difficulty, for
indeed the tray was well supplied. I made an
excellent meal, read a newspaper, and then rung
the bell. A voice again called at the door—" Did
ye's ring, sir !" " Yes," I replied ; " Will you
be pleased to order the chambermaid to bring me a
bed-room candlestick, and warm my bed ?" Paddy
went down stairs, and delivered his message to a
group that appeared to be still discussing the
merits of my true character in the kitchen. The
moment the chambermaid heard the announce-
ment that her services were to be called into requisition, she bolted out of the house, declaring that
she thought the devil was able enough to warm
his own bed, and, for her part, she would have no

hand in it. On this Paddy returned, and said—
" The chambermaid sends her compliments, Mr.
Wizard, and thinks that you'll find yourself quite
warm enough ; and when ye's want to go to bed,
there's a bed-room candlestick on the landing outside of the door, *with your room in it.*" In a
minute or two afterwards I went to the landing-
place, and, as Paddy described, found a candlestick, with a small piece of paper attached, marked
" No. 10, your sleeping-room." It was an old-
fashioned house, as I have already explained, so
that I had a little difficulty in finding No. 10; but
after wandering up-stairs, I was, at length, suc-
cessful in my search ; and being a good deal
fatigued, I got to bed, and fell sound asleep. I got
up in the morning betimes, dressed myself, and proceeded to the door, which opened outwards.—
Having unlocked it, I endeavoured to push it
open, but for a time found this an operation by no
means to be so easily accomplished, for apparently
the inmates of the house, in order to prevent my
getting out, had taken the precaution to pile up,
against the entrance an immense number of chairs,
tables, stools, pots, pans, and other available
utensils. With one lusty drive, however, I

managed ultimately to knock away the barricade, over which I made my way into the kitchen, where I found the worthy priest, Father ——, completing his explanations of the previous night as to my real character and respectability. I need scarcely conclude this anneedote—which is founded on fact—by informing the reader that I neither required bills nor advertisements for that evening's entertainment in Carrick-on-Suir, for the whole village was anxious to know what kind of a devil I was.

THE RUSSIAN CEREMONY

OF

BLESSING THE WATERS,

THE RUSSIAN CEREMONY
OF
BLESSING THE WATERS.

I HAVE already stated in a former sketch, that Saint Petersburgh, the Russian Capital, abounds with a greater number of striking and remarkable sights to attract the eye of the stranger than any other city in Europe. Amongst these, I may mention the august church of Saint Isaac's, and the magnificent ceremony of the blessing of the waters. The former cannot fail to be seen at all times by any one sailing from Constadt to the capital, as its golden dome and minaret tower far above the other buildings of the city, but the ceremony only occurring once a year, and at a particular season, is seldon witnessed by the mere casual visitor to St. Petersburgh Both, however, are well worthy of the attention of the tourist, and cannot fail, when properly appreciated by the spectator, to leave upon the mind a deep and solemn impression. The church of St. Isaac's, although it has been in progress for fifty years, and still unfinished, is one of the most magnificent buildings in Europe, if not in the world. It has four fronts, each of which has its pediment supported by Corinthian pillars. The whole exterior of the Church is of polished Finland granite, and each of the four fronts is formed of twenty-four pillars of the same material, red-coloured and beautifully polished, the base and capital of the several pillars being bronze. On the entablature of every pediment, is a bronze casting, illustrative of some portion of Scripture history— the figures of which are twice the size of life. The entire structure is surmounted by a dome and minarets, which seem to mount up into the clouds and the effect of the whole is grand and imposing. But if the outside of the building is rich and striking

in appearance, what can one say of the interior; it
is at once gorgeous and awe-inspiring. The church
on the inside is supported by one hundred and twenty-
five pillars of malachite, a green stone of immense
value, each column is twenty-five feet in height by
three feet in circumference, with bases and capitals
of solid gold, while the altars, which are covered
with burnished gold, sparkle with thousands of
diamonds. Every part of the immense pile is fitted
up with the same regard to effect, and the cere-
monies of the Russian Greek Church are equally
noted for their pomp and magnificence. One of
these, in connexion with this church, which may be
considered more of a national than a sectarian display, I will endeavour to describe. It is called the
blessing of the waters, and here I may premise that
the Neva, on which the ceremony takes place once
a year, is one of the most beautiful rivers in Europe,
although it wants most of those peculiarities which
are considered essential to such a character. It
forms no cataracts, it is bounded by no rocky shores,
it penetrates no romantic glens, but it has other quali-
ties which more than compensate for their absence.
It has no tide, and therefore leaves no deposits of
mud or shingles behind it. It is subject to no moun-

tain torrents, and does not come down at one time in a turgid flood, nor at another contract its stream into a narrow current winding through banks of dry shingles.   It issues from the Ludage, a lake of pure water, in a large and copious body, pursues its devious way through a rich country, and glides along with majestic volume as transparent as crystal, being at all seasons and at all hours equally clear, equally pure, and equally full until it is lost in the Gulf of Finland.   It is true that on its tranquil waters there are sometimes very destructive and extensive inundations, producing most serious ravages; but these do not arise from the same cause that disturbs other rivers.   It is not the solution of snows or the falling of rains which swell the waters towards its source, and so cause it to come down in rapid torrents, overflowing its banks in their descent.   The reason is found, not above, but below, and the evil originates not at its source, but at its mouth.   The Gulf of Finland, into which it falls, resembles a funnel, wide at its junction with the Baltic, and narrowing to a point where it meets the Neva.   When a westerly wind prevails with any strength, and is continued for some time, the waters of the Gulf are driven back, and swell as the channel contracts, till forming a great barrier at the mouth of the Neva, the issue of its current is obstructed, and its waters, with those of the Gulf are poured down upon the low grounds which form this part of the Channel, so that the evil is not imputed by the Russians to the River, which they adore, but to the Gulf into which it falls.

To shew their respect and veneration for its waters, a solemn and religious ceremony annually takes place, expressly for the purpose of consecrating them. The sixth day of January, old style, commemorates with them three great festivals; the Epiphany or manifestation, the baptism of Christ, and the birthday of the Royal Family, an epoch which the Russians consider of as much importance as the other two. On this day, great preparations are made for the solemn ceremonial, at which I was present, and as I have before observed, it is called the blessing of the waters. I may explain, that there is a small stream named the Moika, which has been formed into a canal, and it communicates with the larger river through a magnificent arch which connects the hermitage (the Emperor's Picture Gallery) with the winter palace. Here a large platform was erected over the stream, and an octagon temple was placed upon it. The temple was open at both sides, and ornamented with carved and gilded cherubims and other similar figures. On four sides were pictures representing the " Preaching of John in the Wilderness ;" the " Miraculous Draught of Fishes :" the " Passage of the Red Sea ;" and the " Baptism of Christ in the Jordan." In the centre of the temple, the floor was open, and a flight of steps were let down to the ice, in which was cut a square hole, that the waters of the Moika might be seen to mingle with those of the Neva below, and above was suspended a golden dove in the centre of gilded rays, hovoring over the sacred spot, and the mingled waters were called the Jordan. About 12 o'clock in the forenoon an immense crowd was collected on the quays, and on the ice a broad passage was left from the door of the winter palace to the temple, which is spread on these occasions with the most gorgeous carpeting. About 1 o'clock, a procession which had assembled within was seen to issue from it. First came two priests in rich vestments, bearing swallow-tailed banners, followed by another holding a lantern with a huge wax light on the end of a pole. Then came a train of about three hundred priests, some bearing

ccclesiastical banners, some tapers, and others books. They
immediately preceded the Patriarch, or Metropolite, as he is
now called, with all the Bishops
of the Greek Church, dressed in
snow-white robes. And here I

must admit that never did I look upon mortal being so saintly in appearanee as the Metropolite. He possessed a heavenly open countenance, with silver beard and long flowing silver hair, and his costume was of the most gorgeous description. On his vest_ ments were embroidery of gold and diamonds, and the mitre on his head seemed laden with diamonds, one of which, I understand, was valued at a hundred thousand silver rubles. His entire aspect was truly commanding and sublime, and such as was fitted to produce upon members of the Russian Greek Church a feeling of adoration. After the Bishops, there followed in the procession the whole of the Emperor's suite, the Court choristers chaunting hymns and carrying banners, keys of citadels, and other trophies of war, in the midst of which a stranger could almost instinctively say that that commanding figure, although in a simple garb, when compared with that of his suite, (a plain military uniform), was Nicoli, Emperor of Russia. A long train of officers of the Court came after his Majesty, all in splendid dresses; and at one of the windows of the winter palace, of which there are 300, sat the Empress and her suite, the others being crowded with different members of the *corps diplomatique.* The weather, I may observe, was intensely cold, the thermometer standing at 40 degrees below the freezing point of Fahrenheit, yet all the parties in the procession had their heads bared, even the Emperor forming no exception, and this example was immediately followed by the immense crowd of ten thousand persons. The priests and common people in Russia suffer their hair to grow intensely thick—the former keep it long, the latter cut it short and square below the ears—and it hangs around them as if they had inverted a wooden bowl on their heads, and it seemed equally impenetrable to the cold. How they managed to protect themselves from the intensity of the cold to which at another time they would think it mortal to expose their bare heads, I cannot say, but I and my companions were very reluctant to do so, until called on frequently by the people about us, and threatened as infidels if we did not comply,   The first effect of the cold upon us was that of burning, as if our heads had been suddenly thrown into a furnace, exemplifying the poetical expression, not fiction, but fact—

> That parching air burns frore,
> And cold performs the effect of fire.

This feeling was succeeded by numbness and loss of all sensation, and we expected to loose our whole heads (as some people did their noses) by mortification of the entire cranium. It was some consolation to us, however, that all our senses, except that of feeling, remained unimpaired, and we continued to hear, see, and smell, as distinctly as ever, though the organs through which sight, sound, and odour were conveyed, seemed to be obliterated.

The procession moved slowly along the platform, where they ranged themselves around the temple. The Patriarch then descended to the aperture on the ice, uttered a solemn prayer, and bending forward through the opening, he addressed the mingling currents, blessed the waters, and conferred upon them every quality that could be useful to man. Then drawing up some from the stream, he sprinkled it on the Emperor, and around on the whole company, who eagerly held their faces forward, to catch a falling drop. At this moment, a signal was given to the fortress on the opposite side, when a discharge of artillery blazed along the ramparts, the choir chaunted aloud an harmonious hymn, and all the multitude bent forward, muttering prayers, crossing themselves, and seemingly

affected with the profoundest adoration. As this
was the day that commemorated the birth of Christ,
this event was next celebrated by a corresponding
ceremony, the waters of the Moika representing
those of the Jordan, and were so called for the purpose. The procession returned to the palace by the
same route, the Patriarch preceeded by a page
carrying a golden basin filled with the blessed
water. The Patriarch held in his hand an orna-
mental bunch of feathers which he ever and anon
dipped into the water, and sprinkled it on the faces
of the multitude as he went along the whole line of
the platform, until he arrived at the door of the
palace, when he sprinkled it on the Empress and
her Court. The fanaticism of the people was such
that mothers brought new-born infants which they
passed through the frozen water, as the worship-
pers of Moloch passed theirs through the fire, to the
imminent peril of the lives of many who sunk in
the intensity of the cold. A priest was stationed
at the aperture of the blessed waters, who dipped
the children into it, when brought by their mothers.
He took them naked by the leg, and plunged them
head foremost through the hole in the ice. On
this occasion, one child, more sturdy than the rest,

in struggling to extricate itself from the painful
sensation, was let go by the priest, and floated away
with the current, when the priest, turning round to
the distracted mother, said, " The Lord giveth and

the Lord taketh away." Give me another. Another
was immediately handed to him, the mother of this
child firmly believing that her offspring was con-
signed to eternal bliss.

I understand, however, that after these accidents,
the Emperor issued an ukase to the effect, that all
children baptized on this day should be secured in
a blanket, and so dipped into the water. As the
procession returned into the palace, the people
rushed forward to occupy their places, thousands
having previously provided themselves with vessels
of various kinds, which they filled from the precious stream, and carried home as a *panacea* for
all moral and physical evils. Many of them
scrambled down to the ice, where they prostrated
themselves, and thrust their heads with such eagerness into the water, that it was necessary to catch
them by the legs, to prevent them being drowned.
Bottles were filled, clothes were steeped, and sent
up to friends above, who could not approach the
spot. These they clutched up eagerly, and sent
round among the people. Some drank the water,
others poured it into their hands or their bosoms,
others enveloped their heads in wet clothes, at the
same time bowing, crossing, and bending the knees,
and praying with the deepest devotion. When this
was done, they had the appearance of the greatest
happiness. Wherever the water had fallen, the
intensity of the cold had immediately frozen it

stiff, so that their hair was clotted with icicles, and the words of the   oet were literally fulfilled :—

Stiriaque impexis pendebant horrida barbis.

Yet they seemed to feel nothing, a glow of enthusiasm was on their faces, and the warmth of their devotion disarmed the intensity of the frost.   Notwithstanding this, I could observe a few who seemed to think very little of the solemnity—paid little attention to the ceremony—and laughed at and ridiculed the eagerness of those who struggled to catch a drop of the blessed water.   They seemed, however, to be the lowest and dirtiest of the crowd, who, like some of the profligate mob in our own country, laugh at all religion as superstition; but the great body of the decent and religious citizens regarded it as a most serious and solemn ceremony, and were profoundly affected by it.

PROFESSOR

ANDERSON

AT

BALMORAL CASTLE.

FROM THE
Note Book of the Wizard of the North.

PROFESSOR
ANDERSON
AT
Balmoral Castle.

———o———

HERE are a few inci-
dents connected with
my invitation and jour-
ney to Balmoral, to
perform before her Majesty and the Court, in addition
to those already mentioned in the newspapers, which
I think may be set down in my note-book for the
amusement of the reader: not that I consider the
circumstances in themselves of that importance to
entitle them to be regarded in the light of material
for entertaining history, but rather as affording an

illustration of the ignorance and superstition which
still prevails amongst the common people in the
Highlands of Scotland. I may premise by observing that in this part of the country, where the
royal presence and its every proceeding was regarded with the deepest interest by the inhabitants,
there were many and grave speculations as to the
Queen's command to the Wizard of the North to
perform in her royal presence at Balmoral, and on
this point it is no exaggeration to state that some
of the "unco guid" thought very little of her Majesty for the compliment she was about to pay to
one whom they shrewdly guessed had dealings of
some sort with that much dreaded personage whom
Milton has panegyrized as the " Prince and chief of
many throned powers."

As I have formerly informed the reader, the
village of Kincardine O'Neil, near the banks of the
Dee, is the birth-place of the Wizard of the North,
and here, even at the present day, the belief in
witchcraft and things supernatural, prevails with a
strength and vigour which it will take many years
of study and cultivation to eradicate. On my way
to Balmoral, I passed through the primitive clachan
where I had not once been from my boyhood, and
at which I stopped to make certain inquiries, the
result of which are of no particular interest to any
one but the writer. Here I found that my Wizard's
reputation had been invested with a somewhat
equivocal kind of fame, and that the belief in my
connexion with diabolical agency was fully con-
firmed by the recollection of certain prophetic fore-
bodings that had been given utterance to at my
birth, and the memory of which still lived in the
minds of the old people of the parish. In my early
days, I may explain, marriages and births in Kincardine O'Neil, were invariably attended by what
are called cairds or spae-wives—poor people who

went about the country as beggars, and who, on these festive occasions always managed, by a display of their professional skill (which was generally directed towards prophesying good fortune to those whose bounty they were to enjoy), to obtain a liberal share of the good things provided for the entertainment. One of their fraternity, it seems, called at the house of my father on the morning of my birth, and after having satisfied herself with all the particulars as to the precise time the lad was born, with other attendant circumstances, commenced to read my horoscope, in the course of which she foretold that the bairn would travel through many foreign lands, see strange faces, and come into personal converse with kings and queens. In those days the spirit of emigration had made little progress amongst the Highlanders, compared to what it has done since, and the people in the locality to which my father belonged had an idea that no one should ever quit his native soil, unless he had offended against the laws of his country, and therefore my worthy parent being a believer in this logic, regarded the story of the spae-wife as an insult to the credit of the family. The addition besides of the anticipated conversations with kings and queens was, in his eyes, so great an outrage upon truth, that he summarily ejected the offender from his house. The old dame, whose name was Elspath Dodds, blazoned her wrongs over the parish, imprecated wrath upon the devoted head of my poor father, and insisted the more strenuously that he should yet live to see her words fulfilled—one part of the poor creature's prophecy, by the bye, which, I regret to say, was not implemented, as my father died when his family were but young in years. Strange, however, and yet not more strange than true, the old spae-woman's predictions, in my case, have been curiously and strikingly fulfilled. I have lived a chequered but eventful life, and have had many reverses of fortune. I have travelled in every country in Europe—seen surprising sights, and come in contact with curious faces—performed in courts, conversed with kings aud queens, and have received more tokens of royal favour and kingly patronage than any other man, be he Duke, Lord, Earl, Marquis. Count, Prime Minister, or Professor of Magic, in Christendom.

From the facts just referred to, added to the circumstance, that it was previously known I intended to visit Kincardine O'Neil on the road from Aberdeen to Balmoral, my presence excited almost as much speculation as the Queen, whose message I was hastening to obey. When the coach, on which I was an outside passenger, stopped to change horses at the village, a crowd had assembled, and eager inquiries were at once set on foot as to which of the passengers was the far-famed Wizard. Unfortunately, the coachman, with whom I had not been the least communicative during the journey, had been present at some of my exhibitions in Aberdeen. He recognised my features, and, in answer to the questions as to which was the Wizard, was not slow in pointing out the person of your humble servant for the inspection of the onhangers. I need not say how I inwardly anathematized the fellow for his impertinence, but the thing was done, and could not be helped, so I put the best possible face on the matter, and looked almost as pleased as if I had been reaping a benefit. For a time the crowd contented themselves with staring at me, as if I had been a wild animal, and confined their remarks to whispers and pantomimic gestures, to indicate that they were satisfied I was something human; but, at length, one old woman, with spectacles on nose, who had gazed at me for a minute or two in open-monthed astonishment,

could restrain herself no longer, but, addressing me, lustily called out, "Come awa doon, Jock Anderson, and let y'er auld aunt look at y'er feet, for I hae nae seen ye since the day ye war born, when Elspeth Dodds spaed yer fortin." This speech was not more unexpected than it was amusing to me and the rest of the passengers. I now saw that any farther attempt at disguise would be fruitless; so descended from my seat, stepped down amongst the motley group assembled around the vehicle, and after shaking hands with the venerable dame who had so unceremoniously introduced herself to my notice, found that she was in reality my father's sister, whom I had never before set

eyes upon. I need scarcely say, the old lady, upon
examination, found that neither of my feet were
cloven, nor very much unlike other folks; and that
I very soon satisfied her that the deevil's cantrips
I had to play before the Queen, of which she expressed herself terribly afraid, were perfectly
harmless and natural. My kind and loving aunt,
who seemed quite an oracle in her way for putting
all manner of inconsiderate questions, began to
remonstrate with me upon the sinfulness of my
Wizard profession, and I was about to return the
compliment by some reflections upon the super-
stitious notions of the ignorant, when the guard
told me the horses were ready, and I was obliged
to leave my newly-found relative in the same frame
of mind with regard to my unholy calling as I had
found her, but with this difference, that I managed
to transport from my own pocket to her's a five
pound note, whose presence there, amongst the
other valuables which it contained. I have no doubt
she would afterwards ascribe to something else than
the effects of natural magic. With this interrup-
tion, we resumed our journey by Tulloch and Ballater
to Crathie. I arrived at Crathie, which is a short
distance from Balmoral, on Saturday, and proceeded
to the inn there, highly delighted with the prospect
of the honor about being conferred on me by performing before her Majesty. I ought to mention, however, that I had some days before taken the precaution to send forward an agent to secure apartments for me in this same Highland hotel, and that
the whole of my luggage and travelling apparatus
had been there awaiting my arrival. My messenger,
it turned out, had taken the rooms for me as
"Mr. Anderson from Aberdeen," and then went on
to Balmoral to make some other necessary arrange-
ments. The landlord, it subsequently appeared,
with a curiosity common to his class, was not con-

tented with the simple address given him by my
agent, but had commenced to busy himself in ex-
amining my luggage, the large quantity and strange
shape of some parts of which excited his suspicion
that a' wasna richt, and his fears and anxieties on
this head were not much allayed when, on decy-
phering the engraved plates on some of my boxes,
he made out the ominous words, " Wizard of the
North." The result of this discovery was, that on
reaching the inn door, and inquiring of one of the
inmates if apartments had been taken here for
Mr. Anderson of Aberdeen, I was stared at for
about half a minute by the servant girl, who, after
eyeing me with a half comic, half puzzled expression of face, shouted "No," and then made the
best of her way out of the inn by a back entrance.
Being somewhat cold and hungry with my long ride
on the top of a coach in these Highland latitudes, I
was in no humour for playing at bo-peep with any
one, so noticing a part of my performing furniture
in the lobby, "I made bold to enter," as Paddy
would say, walked up stairs to an apartment on the
first flat, I supposed to the dining-room, and rung
the bell for dinner. I had not been long in this
place, when I heard a whispering of voices on the
staircase, and the sound as of a number of parties
pushing each other forward to the door of the room
where I was sitting, on which I said, " Come away,
landlord, and let us have some dinner." I had
guessed aright as to the party at the door, for in
stepped mine host, followed by the landlady and a
posse of domestics, with as much terror depicted on
their countenances as if I had proposed to make a
meal of the whole establishment, when mine host
had stared at me for some time, and scanned
me carefully from head to heel, he exclaimed,
"Na, na, Mr. Aunerson, or whatever else ye ca'
yourself, I hae heard o' yer deevil's tricks and

witcheries afore ye cam, and ye'll get nae dinner
here.   There's nane o' yer deevil's cleek will put up
in my hoose, sae gang yer gate, and tak' yer Wizard
furniture alang wi' ye."   Surprised and angry with
this extraordinary reception, I told the landlord I
was in no disposition to put up with any of his impu-
dence, and that the sooner he gave up this non-
sense and got ready some dinner for his customer the
better it would be for him and his household.   I
was proceeding to enforce my demands by other
arguments of a more pacific character, when the
landlady struck in, and insisted on my leaving the
inn, saying, Mr. Johnson, of Glasgow, had told
them the kind o' character I was before I cam', and
the whole of the servants were so much afraid that
they would not stay in the house a single night if I
persisted in remaining.'   "And," added Boniface,
by way of support to his better half, "we hae
loaded a' the guns i' the hoose with siller saxpences,
so ye see, Mr. Wizard, we are prepared for you."
Being now completely out of temper with this ill
usage, I swore I would not leave the premises on
any account.   I insisted it was a public inn, and
that as a traveller they must supply me with
refreshments.   On this I resolutely resumed my
seat, and resolved to abide with firmness the issue
of the adventure, when the landlord and his party
beat a retreat to the kitchen, from which they commenced unceremoniously to toss my boxes, bundles,
and valuable apparatus into the high road.   Hearing
the clatter raised by the falling of my luggage, I
rushed down stairs to the rescue, and proceeded to
uplift and replace my soiled bags and shattered
boxes, when I was met by about a dozen Highlanders, including the ostler, stable-boy, the boots,
and the whole available force about the inn—who
had armed themselves with pitchforks, knives,
broom-besoms, and a couple of old fowling-pieces—

with which they advanced upon me, headed by
the landlord, swearing dreadful oaths, and calling on
me to surrender. In the midst of the uproar
which ensued, I had seized upon a clothes-pole

that stood in the door-way, and like Quixote of old,
resolved to defend myself, if necessary, against a
whole army of such wretches, when a party of
gentlemen came up to inquire the cause of the
disturbance. On looking round, I discovered
amongst the number no less a personage than my
Lord John Russell, along with the minister of the
parish, and two or three members of her Majesty's
household, who had come in this direction for their
afternoon walk, and who seemed quite anxious to

ascertain the cause of the affray. The minister of
the parish, who was well known to Boniface, advanced up to my warlike opponents, and com-
manded them to lay down their weapons, requesting
me, at the same time, to explain the occasion of
this hostile demonstration. Rejoiced with a deli-
verance so unexpected, I briefly stated my case,
interrupted by many explanations from the landlord
and his wife; upon which the worthy clergyman
took my part, informed the landlord I was journey-
ing on her Majesty's service, and ordered him without delay to convey my luggage into the inn, from
which it had been ejected, at the same time giving
his security that he would be answerable that the
Wizard, during his stay, would play off none of his
cantrips upon the landlord or any of his household.
On hearing that I was on my way to the Queen,
Mine host changed his tone and aspect entirely, called
upon his domestics to lay aside their weapons of
offence, and help to replace the *gentleman's* luggage.
Boniface humbly apologized to me for his rudeness,
and I, thanking my deliverer for his interference, re-
entered the inn, from one of the windows of which
I could see the clergyman walking over to where the
Premier and his party stood. They all enjoyed a
hearty laugh at the expense of the unfortunate
Wizard, whose awkward adventure, I afterwards
learned, gave immense amusement to the Queen
and Court. After this, matters got on pretty
smoothly for a day or two between Bonnets and I,
until an accident occurred which caused me to be
again ejected from the inn, and apprehended on
suspicion of theft. My friend Johnson, who is a
bit of a wag in his way, had, it appears, told Boniface
some wonderful stories about the Wizard's powers
in the transmutation of metals, and cautioned him
to be careful as to where he kept his siller, as by a
wave of the professor's magic wand it could be

made to fly to any distance, or mayhap be trans-
formed into some beast or bird, such as the doves,
geese, or guinea pigs which I carried along with
me. The landlord, I observed, who watched my out-
goings and incomings with considerable suspicion,
stood particularly in dread of the guinea pigs.
Believing the absurd stories with which Johnson
contrived from time to time to frighten him, Boniface
had caused his wife to take his cash out of the
muckle kist, where it had always been safely deposited until my arrival, and got it sewed up into one
of the pillows of his own bed for greater security.
It so happened about this time that the inn was
filled with travellers, for one of whom it had been
necessary to make a "shake doon" bed in lieu of
better accommodation. When the chamber-maid
was ordered to make up a bed for the stranger, she
was rather at a loss for pillows, so contrived to
borrow one from her master's apartment, and un-
luckily selected that in which the bank-notes of
mine host were firmly sewed and securely deposited.
Nothing was heard of this mistake until Boniface
and his wife retired to rest for the night, where,
upon lifting up the pillows, they found that the
precious one was awanting. Mine host, who could
bellow like a bull-calf on the slightest occasion, and
generally exercised his powers of voice on every
opportunity, without making further inquiries, at
once set up a howl *for the loss of his siller*, not unlike an Indian's war-whoop, which soon aroused
every soul in the establishment. The alarm was
instantly conveyed to the inmates of the kitchen;
The landlord declared the devil had been at his wark,
and, in spite o' saint or minister, the Wizard must
be placed in safe custody until some one went for
his friend, Laird M'Taggart, the nearest Justice of
the Peace, who resides some eight or ten miles off.
I was just in the act of getting into bed, equally

astonished with the rest of the inmates as to the
cause of the unearthly disturbance I had heard,
when the room was roughly entered by the landlord

and his servants. They, in spite of my remon-
strances and entreaties, seized hold of my arms,
which they pinioned, and then marched me down
stairs in triumph to the coach-house. I was without coat, hat, or other covering but my trousers,
and must have cut rather an odd-looking figure,
guarded by Boniface, calling upon me to give up the
"bawbees and the bowster," and applying such
epithets as thief, loon, and imp of the devil. Not
knowing at the time the precise cause of the tumult,
I loudly expostulated against this ungentlemanly
treatment, but all to no purpose—the landlord's blood
was up, and so I had to submit myself to be shut in
the coach-house as a prisoner, the door being locked,

and guarded by several of the Highland kinsmen of my ferocious accuser. I was kept in this place for about two hours, until Boniface arrived, and ordered my immediate liberation. He explained that "it was all a mistake,"—the servant girl had got the bawbees and the bowster,—he offered ten thousand apologies to *his honor's glory* for the false imprisonment. I need not say that I threatened all kinds of revenge for this disgraceful treatment, and an action of damages for defamation and wrong imprisonment—all of which brave intentions, however, soon evaporated over a flowing cup of mountain dew out the landlord's bottle—at the end of which he not only promised me a Highland welcome in all time coming, for the unintentional affront he had put upon me, but added in a confidential tone—" Man, I'll gie ye a ride on my ain pownie up to the head o' Lochnagar, and charge ye nae expenses."

In closing this notice, I may just observe that, however pleasant and profitable in other respects my professional visit to her Majesty at Balmoral turned out afterwards, my journey was made not a little uncomfortable through these exhibitions of Highland superstition.

www.ingramcontent.com/pod-product-compliance
Lightning Source LLC
Chambersburg PA
CBHW081521040426
42447CB00013B/3300